Butcher
Baker
His-Story Maker

"He who kisses the Joy as it flies
Lives in Eternity's sunrise"

— *William Blake*

Published in 2020 by Birdfish Books
www.birdfishbooks.com.au

All rights reserved. No part of this edition
of this text may be reproduced or transmitted
in any form or by any means, electronic
or mechanical, including photocopy, recording
or any informational storage and retrieval system,
without prior permission from the publisher.

Cover images: Bert Leister's dam, Norwood Hill:
Castlemaine Historical Society, Inc., VCMHS 2007 1097;
K Mc & author in the Guildford bush: author's own;
galah by Eric Sheperd; pardalotes and fantail by Elizabeth
Gould; kookaburra by Janet Flinn; rosellas by John Gould;
wattlebird by Neville Cayley.

ISBN-13: 978-0-9953718-6-6

Butcher
Baker
His-Story Maker

*stories from the kitchen,
in-verse*

by Tru S. Dowling

BIRDFISH BOOKS

Author's Note & Acknowledgements

This book is a love song for my father (a swan-song of a bird in flight), twelve years in the making. It is also a repository of his deep love for Castlemaine, its people and bushland, in war and more recent times. It re-imagines my father's childhood memories, gleaned from my own memories and interviews.

Butcher, Baker, His-Story Maker is primarily based on fact, though some parts are not 'true,' (nor do I claim them to be 'Tru'). History is interspersed with the nature of storytelling to form a verse narrative that riffs on personal voices and desires in a wider, wilder world. But when does memory become story? Fiction relies on make-believe alongside verisimilitude. In this spirit, I've occasionally rearranged and melded events and dates, filled gaps and embellished characters, to enhance the narrative flow (particularly parts of Carnival and Blue). Throughout, no disrespect towards family, living or dead, is intended. That said I've tried to be true to the characters, time, and experiences herein, while changing some names as requested. Hopefully this book resonates with and beyond my own desires to hold my father (as author and daughter). He has recently passed, which makes this writing (and reading) an act of grief. Now these stories are passed on to you, the reader, in an act of love. Grief is a strange creature because it honours life; it speaks lyric poetry's language.

Les Murray says 'there is poetry in all language'[i], which poses inquiry, an exchange, a banter of play and meaning, of connection. My father connected with every person he met. He also read people like books, with intuitive openness, expression and joy. He seems to invite us to 'kiss the Joy as it flies'[ii] even more in this season of grief — his voice, his manner, and his heart wing the air of change.

Many friends, family members and colleagues have helped shape these poems, and I'm grateful for their time, interest and expertise.

Firstly, heartfelt thanks to my dear dad, for his trust, generosity and humour in sharing his stories with me (and my family); this book would not exist and I would not be a writer without him. I offer sincere gratitude to Dr Sue Gillett whose astute suggestions supported first drafts, and to Birdfish publisher Tegan Gigante for her gentle, logical approach to making this book finally live in print. Castlemaine Word Mine poetry group — Rob Wallis, Ann de Hugard, Annie Hunter, Allis Hamilton, Sam Bews, Cath James, Tegan Gigante, Andy Jackson, Rachael Wenona Guy, Kate Seppings, Ross Donlon, Sue Flanagan, and Julie Begg — your insightful feedback has honed these poems across years, along with Bendigo writers Beck Sutton and Mary Pomfret, and London poet extraordinaire, Katherine Gallagher. I offer particular gratitude for Drs Ian Irvine, Sue King-Smith, Chris Wallace-Crabbe, and Anne Elvey's considered care, time and edits. Love and appreciation especially go to my family, my children, and my husband and partner in life, John. You know your value in honouring these story gifts.

Some of these poems (in earlier versions) have appeared in anthologies and journals:
Climbing (Flight IV), won the Francis Webb Award, Poetica Christi Press poetry competition, published in *Taking Flight* (PCP), and online, *Eureka Street, vol 22, no 5,* 2012.
Dismantling Kitchen (Mouth to Mouth, I-III), *Scintillae*, Bendigo Tafe, 2012.
Harvest 2 (Cyclops II) and *Superb Mates* (Blue II), *Painted Words*, Bendigo Tafe, 2016.
Model Making (Icarus IV), *Painted Words*, Bendigo Tafe, 2017.
An Offering for Sister Omar (Offerings III), *Tamba 60th Anniversary Edition*, Goulburn Valley Writers' Group, Inc., 2017.

Some poems were part of featured performances across various events and venues from 2010-2019, including Mark Time poets' readings, Castlemaine Poetry Readings, and Poeticas, Castlemaine; Newstead Short Story Tattoo: *Sisters' Salon*, and Words in Winter: *Namaste*, Newstead; Chamber Poets, Woodend; Ballan Writers Community presenters' readings, Ballan; The Write Stuff, Bendigo Writers' Festivals, Bendigo Tafe, La Trobe Arts Symposium:

Once Upon a Future, and Write on the Fringe Festivals, Bendigo; Torriano's Monthly Poets' Series, London (UK):
Footage for my Father (Songs from the Kitchen, *Prologue*), *An Offering for Sister Omar* (Offerings III), *Harvest 1 & 2* (Cyclops I & II), *Climbing* (Flight IV), *Model Making* (Icarus IV), *Superb Mates* (Blue II), *Carnival Clowns* (Carnival I), *Cooked Books* (Silence in the Kitchen, Dialogue 3), *The Song is a Sign* (Flight II), and *Filching Acoustics* (Flight III).

Thank you to publishers, directors and judges for their support.

Photographs and documents are used with kind permission from Keith, Graeme, and Clare McShanag, the Castlemaine Historical Society, Inc., and the author's private collection.

[i] Quote from Murray's speech at a forum during Mildura Writers' Festival, 2008.
[ii] Quote from William Blake's poem, *Eternity*.

Contents

weight

> Songs from the Kitchen *(Prologue)* ... 15
> Icarus ... 18
> Blood ... 21
> Labyrinth ... 24
> Rabbits ... 27
> Mum's Girl *(Dialogue 1)* ... 30
> Labour ... 31
> Chain ... 35
> Offerings ... 38

flood

> Heroes at the Table *(Dialogue 2)* ... 47
> Laps ... 49
> Carnival ... 50
> Blue ... 52

flight

> Musings from the Nest *(Monologues 1&2)* ... 59
> Flight ... 61
> Shell ... 65
> Cloud ... 67

sacrifice

> Flames ... 73
> Wick ... 76
> Silence in the Kitchen *(Dialogue 3)* ... 78
> Dante ... 79
> Resurrecting the Narrator *(Dialogue 4)* ... 80
> Delivery ... 82
> Cyclops ... 84
> Spacemaster ... 87
> Incalculable ... 91
> A Pre-dawn Collision *(Monologue 3)* ... 94

ether

> Stories from the Ashes *(Epilogue)* ... 99
> Mouth to Mouth ... 102

Notes ... 107

Appendix ... 113

*for K. Mc.
and all the storytellers
with love and gratitude*

– *Castlemaine, 2011*

Songs from the Kitchen *(Prologue)*

Rhythms long as memory burst
from my father's lips - poems
stories, movies, stars
glitter still. The radio blares
through the day, drones all night,
a backdrop score
inking life with its beats.

From the din of the past, over
and over, phrases repeat, drift,
warp like the weft
of a wing changing
direction with the wind.

We sit in Dad's kitchen not three
miles from Norwood Hill,
right by Barker's Creek
where Rasmussen's Bakery stood.
We eat buttered Boston Bun and sip
tea steaming from cups like a genie.

He speaks and sings the forgotten things,
timbre resonates over mosquito radio.
I start to record
as he conjures beloved Banjo:
*'Twas Mulga Bill from Eaglehawk that caught
the cycling craze.* Rising up – hand on heart,
the other flung to kingdom come –
he booms.   Stature switches,
flour-grey hair falls across an eyebrow
craggy as a Scottish heath. Palms together
for a prayer to Saint Francis. Lids close,
tongue clicks and he sighs to a smile, and we're . . .

riding ten miles in the rain and the hail
to Harcourt to pick apples for ten bob a week;

I was eldest of five in a house full of boys,
my father carved carcasses for bread,
we lived off the dead,
and Mum's home-made jam before bed,

a pause . . . his brow rises,
tone, a semi-quaver lower,

from my third grade reader, in the dead of night,
the Hobyars came running, yes, run, run, running,
catching little dog Dingo, and eating, yes eating!

The quinces we picked
over the back yard fence, and pelted at birds
to pinch their eggs,

and all the while, words
leap and prance as light
fills the room. He skips across
time from scene to scene, plucks
memories like movies that grew
his dreams:

Random Harvest, The Razor's
Edge, Hobson's Choice, Born
Yesterday, Tarzan, and Shane:
his *Boys' Own* image
stared back from the screen as its silver
lined his fist-filled pockets; fighter
pilots dared him into the war,

bug-eyed.   Now
both hands stretch wide.
Baritone explodes

Oh Danny Boy . . . the room, my focus, pans
to pipes attuned to recalling
when he first knew what he wanted,
when he first flew in the clouds
of his childhood home.

– *Norwood Hill, 1942*

Icarus

I.
Ken propels legend into action.
He is Icarus above the waves, arms
stiff as two rulers
gliding through the lounge
of their four-roomed family home. A machine gun
throttles from the back of his throat.
He lands with a stu-stu-stutter, pores over
aircraft in the history-thick book. Learns how
to construct whalebone ribs, wings that outstretch skies.
A Jonah, he climbs inside.

II.
He thinks of his father, grounded but gone
legging sheep in the city or cycling up to Bendigo
to slaughter for Manpower. He wonders
how his father slits each carcass, how strange it is
to feel the sheer weight of it
while the animal hangs there
waiting to cure.

III.
Next Saturday, Ken's at the flicks
with Mum, her belly a globe
in her lap. Newsreels report –
Thousands of our Nation's beloved sons
have joined Spitfire squadrons taking off
from the Mother land. They'll cross
the Indian ocean and drop
missiles on the enemy invaders. Ken glares
as scenes jump. Propellers swarm, wings glide,
whistles fall through the endless sky,
breaking falsetto.

His mother thanks God
for her eldest beside her,
for Frank's keen cutting skills. *God Save
the King* blares over the speaker
across the picture theatre's crowded
silhouettes. The heads and shoulders all in a row
remind him of shooting gallery ducks
at the show.

IV.
After school the following week,
Mum's at the line and Ken's on a mission.
He comes from the shed with an armful
of wood.   *My boy's a birdman
inside and out*, Mum tut-tuts,
her hands reach high, pegging
sheets that sail the breeze.

Ken designs flight paths
from off-cuts. Each piece,
from wing-tips to nose to wedge-tailed rudder,
carefully chosen
for glide consistency,
gradient,
predicted radius.

He starts constructing a Tiger Moth.
Its parallel wings magnify a dragonfly's,
with fiddly guns that ride propellers.
Scoring balsa, precision slips,
grain blooms red. Ken holds his place
by sheer grit. His idea unwilling
to bend to the material's flimsy will.

He presses, waits for
gaps to glue together. The smell
of horse guts evaporates

in the bones of this new animal
set to part the wind with its desire for heights.
A single configuration away from angels,
these angles about to spin into light.

Mock engine crescendos, in back yard
runway pitch and dip. Such trickster moves
deny gravity, drive his trajectory – the hand letting go.

It's flying! It's flying!
The plane quivers like a javelin
wrestling resistance mid-air.

That'll be me one day, he breathes.

Blood

I.
His father's boots are caked
with dried blood. Mum states
*Take them off
at the back door!* Frank's face
a storm-eye quietening. *Vi,
the dog'll go crazy. You **know** that.*
She drags the leg
from its cardboard box. She rinses,
slathers dripping; sunset falls
over the marbled rind
of two-tooth. Vi

slides it into the oven, hitches the catch
and turns to load embers
with pinecones Ken gathered
this blue-legged morning by the railway track
half a mile away . . .

chga-cha, chga-cha, chga-cha . . .
Father's boots scuff across the lino, smearing
a trail of prehistoric art. He eyeballs the kids
who hang back at first then lurch
hungry with questions
fighting for first taste

of his first word. And Mum's
getting on all fours, to dilute
the blood stains with bicarb, the stench
with vinegar, scrubbing back and again,
back and again. Her apron balloons
rosebuds on a florid sea, where veins
maroon under-currents in the gull-grey mold.

II.
There's a photograph of the family
butchery on the kitchen wall.
*My grandfather's kindness broke
the butchery business*, Dad suddenly
turns to Ken, speaks in a voice grave
as Sister Eymard's in maths.

They stare at the men *circa 1914*. In sepia,
in their prime, his dad's father
and grandfather alongside another worker.
Arms crossed, the men stand, stiff
in uniforms: white coats and striped aprons
blood-spattered, solemn
as any scientist or doctor. Frankenstein
flickers in Ken's brain. He twitters,
steals a sideways glance. Did
his father hear him?

He stares at the scene, the vertical lines:
corrugations above and pickets beside
what could-have-been
a family home with its lace-eyed windows
comforting bricks. Beneath the verandah,
a washing line of carcasses hung like bestial conkers.
Each cadaver stretched as if chasing
a win or sprinting from an invisible foe.
He knows the blood-stink
of his dad's boyhood, has breathed
the same cloying pungency
that attracts flies to shackled meat.

*You know, before those greedy punters begged
a cut-price, the family
had their own killing yards
and three carts for delivery.*
Dad sounds far away,
his lips in an upside-down smile.
*You could do worse
than to take up the trade*, he says
after a time as if to himself.

Two carts are visible, the wheels slotted
between forefathers and shopfront,
horses heads blurred in sudden movement,
spooked by the flash, perhaps.

Labyrinth

I.
Mum shoos the boys out for the arvo.
They run for the Hill, follow a gully
tunnelling through scrub to the Ajax Mines
where a natural watercourse once
carved out a landslide of miniature cliffs.
Norwood Hill tailings
were rich pickings back then.

Ken and his brothers, Kevin and Mickey,
brush past bush doused in gold. They scramble
over the edge, dirt crumbles like flour.
Cool to touch, damp.
Could be the old man's back,
sweat trickling on clay on a stinking day
at the Abattoir. His mates, missing
across the Pacific or Indian ocean. Could be
trenches at the Front.

Leaf-rot clumps,
rank as old blood. Sticks crack
with each step. Crow, butcher, bower birds
echo Dad's pipe-dry cough
taking off. Their sounds fill blanks
left, questions unspoken.
Getting on with it doesn't make sense.
Mates, there. Dad, here.
Ken pokes at bull ant hills,
dividing rivers of black.

Did they ache
for home like Dad ached to go?
Did each lift an arm or face
and stare into space
at the thought, before
smoothing a blade, assuming
a firm grip on a wood-worn butt,
to raise and aim at flesh
marked or camouflaged
in a slaughter yard or foreign field?
How did killing feel?

II.
The three boys meet up
with the gang from school, Ronny,
Ken Brady and Bubby Cartwright, all
scoot through the labyrinth, skip
rocks, grab fallen branches
to shoulder-cock and pummel
each other. Tommy-gun hunting
instant enemies, they tag and fire:
eh-eh-eh-eh-eh-eh-eh-eh
– *you're dead!*
They grab at dangling roots,
scramble up and roll out on the flat
to better sight each other,
then scat for dear life.

Ken and Mickey grow
radar ears, all the better
to trace shouts scuffling
in the dust of their boots.

III.
The dam on the Hill winks.
Eucalypts strangle
the sky black. Grasses
tussle undulations.

The crew stop to watch
'roos peel hind legs in slow
motion – lope, graze, lope,
huff and *whiff*, heads up,
ears twitch on a rustle.
Bobtails flash through bulrushes.

Ken straddles barbed wire
first, foot catches a hole
and he lands ankle-heavy.
Kevin and Mick go stacks-on-the-mill
feigning help, then the whole bloomin'
lot squeal and grunt in the dirt.

Their dead weight
suffocates. He does the scrum,
squirms out jumping up,
head down.   At a glance,
stars puncture the night's armour.
Warren-weary, Solomon's secrets
abandoned, they're losing the battle
to find a way home.

Rabbits

I.
Rolling from bed, the McKinnon boys
prise sleep from bloodshot eyes.
What are weekends for
but taking out the ferret and dog
to score some rabbits and muck about?

Fog dubs the dawn. Fingers of sun
creep over frost. Hidden squawks
make Ken, Mickey and Kevin
crane their necks, throw their bikes
to scale granite outcrops.
Bent-kneed wattles lean into
the next paddock. Timmy lags
from a leg cocked, pants after
a dozen mysterious smells, startles
a spray of galahs.

They head down to the flats
of Muckleford Creek, where water
puckers grey-green
through a shroud of willows. The fog
thins. Jacko snores inside his box
slapping rhythmic against Ken's hip.

Timmy jumps at gnats, tail and tongue
flailing. He runs ahead chasing bucks
after does, hungry for the hunt.
Ken wrestles nets over
a lotto of holes, ferret box
empty on the bank. His brothers
sit and watch tadpoles scribble
in another language.

II.
Jacko's awake. His ferret face,
keen as a whippet's
gone slightly crazy – head bobbing
in the morning sun.
His pelt shines piebald, ice and steel.
Ken strokes him, whiffs a compost
of gone-off orange and unwashed dog.
Scoops him up, holds warm
underbelly palpitating,
his breath, sour-milk down wind.

Back on the ground,
Jacko's horseshoe stretch
is a lucky sign! Ken takes the cue,
tickles his muzzle
and starts to sing *A King* to him:
A King Jacko a King,
A Lion Jacko a Lion
Forget your dreamin'
We're huntin' vermin
A Lion Jacko a Lion
A King Jacko a King

Jacko springs with each new *King*.
The boys join in (to egg him on):
You're a King, You're a Lion,
Now get those bunnies,
go get 'em, get in!
But from the river bank,
black holes gape at
the King-turned-jester
hard at work chasing his tail!

Below, kittens scuffle in the very burrows
that glove their escape. Instinct
jostles with dirt, fur, breath,
the thigh-thumping
itch of the wait.   *Poor little buggers*
trapped in their trenches, Ken says,
but all's fair in love
and war.   The game
feeds whole families.
Rabbit stew for tea, skins ten
for two 'n six to make hats
for the soldiers, dosh for the flicks.

— *Castlemaine, 2011*

Mum's Girl *(Dialogue 1)*

'I was Mum's girl
you know. Since there were
no girls I was it! The eldest
and the guinea pig! Had to sweep
the floor and do the dishes and get
the boys ready for school, do all
the housework while Mum
was away.'

'So you did the cooking too?'

'Oh yes, Mum taught me to cook.
Gerry was only two, so I had to stay
home to look after him. Skipped school. Dad
didn't do a thing, though he had to work
of course. Yeah, Mum did it tough, but I
helped her. The others wouldn't
lift a finger.

I was the eldest, you see. Mum had all
us boys. Five boys. And now I've got you
four girls. And two boys of course. Now
I'm surrounded by you women,
ruling me!'

– *Norwood Hill, 1942*

Labour

I.
Roll your sleeves and let's get started.
Mum's on at Ken to scrub the dirt
and dice the spuds.

But it's just gone ten! It's Saturday!
We've only just got home!

Slice the carrots to add some colour,
mum says. Blade thuds on wood, blank
as mood, he carves veggie coins.
Turnips have an earthy scent
like weeds pulled from the patch.

The rabbits'll keep, Mum yells
out back. She's gone
to fetch the shin from the safe,
shoos a halo of autumn fly-fizz.
She walks in, glistening
gelatinous as the shank bone.

She holds it
steady, trims the fat;
sinews web blood-streaked flesh.
She dunks the meat, waits awhile.
Then bubble trouble bubble pop!
Steam smears. Her face disappears.

Foam climbs edges frothed as spit,
a taste sated in onion reek.
Meat falls off bone in chunky drifts,
thickening the mix.   Short days lit

in southern light. Wood poke, fire stoke,
stove iron hisses and cracks hotter to test
the pot. Mum sips a spoonful now and then
(a mouthful warms a gutful) through
all the simmer-long day,
instructs him.

Skim the surface carefully, to separate
scunge from steam. Fish out
the bone and leave the veg,
a treat for Tim. He can't come in.
Screen door creaks. Timmy yowls.
Ken's forearms bristle outdoors in May.
Tim's a king but he can't come in,
Mum warns from her kitchen cave.

But whimpering, Tim slips in,
scrambling round the kitchen, crazed.
The chairs upend, the china smashes!
Oh Lord! Look at the muddy prints!
Kevin, Mickey, get a move on,
or your hide'll taste this ladle.
The kettle's on quick smart. Mum huffs,
Tim's a king, but He Can't Come In!

Ken stirs and stirs the rheumy stew,
a figure eight then round and round,
slurps a taste at intervals, listens to
the clock tick, pot pop, the day slowing down.
Clear economy pans out –
from bench to pot to stove to sink,
dished up to table waiting, set;
the kids fidget, anticipate
Dad's hurrump, Mum sits last,
Thank the Lord,
they finally
eat.

II.
Something nags sleep from her,
drags through her lower back.
Vi's belly tightens into mattress sag,
blankets bearing down. A warm
wet rush. *It's time*, she says
to the moonlight seeping
through curtains. Familiar pain
resurges. Her face concertinas.
She turns and tugs
at Frank's flannel back. Swings a leg
into iced air, levering weight. Time
to leave Ken in charge. But Vi's torn
by niggling labour,
feels for the one left
to deal with the little 'uns, and snaps
at Frank who's pushing her. He shrugs
a coat over her shoulders,
*Heave ho, here we go, Vi. I'll have to
be off, directly*, and trundles
(just the same) towards the door.

She snatches sheets
smelling brackish as dam water,
bundles an armful out to the wash-house,
doubles back, pops a head in to the boys'
room. *It's time, Ken. We're leaving
for the hospital* – she grabs the door
as another wave hits – *you know what to do*.

Frost nips at faces. Clock ticks
a heart-beat. Thud thud clammy
feet on lino down the hall
to the kitchen, empty
except for the front door click.
Ken's up with a song tickling
the darkness. He stokes coals, stacks wood,

makes and packs the boys' lunches, and Dad's
already walking back in, shuffling newspapers,
waiting for his tea 'n toast.
Outside, milk cart tinkle and creak.

But Kevin's after Ken's bird eggs, daring
a brawl and Mick's wagging a shoelace
at Timmy's jowl and Gerry's got porridge
slopped in his curls and slopped on the floor
and stares Ken down to mop it up. *C'mon boy,
heave-ho*, Dad grumbles. Ken wishes
they'd all heave-ho, but oh no!
Here you go, Ken, mothering brothers and father
just the same towards the door.

– *Melbourne, 1943*

Chain

I.
Next, Frank greets the sheep
carcass moving down the line.
He silently dissects its geometry: a map
of cuts for week night meals, might be chump
chops, a leg roast, or shank
stew – his brood waiting
at the Castlemaine train for him
on Fridays, like a food queue.

First he grips the hind shin, fingers boning knife
to score fat. A wrist-flick slides the long curve
of calf-bone to thigh, his wife's
naked shape flashes in the half-light. Ache
pushed into absence, forces
blade into flesh. The skun cloak
shrugs in a heap, off the belt
to his feet, falling just before
the severed leg.   *Next*

punches another
casualty down the line.
Swings the chain.
The long-armed lug of another
hefts rump cheek
to his embrace. The timer's ticking
with each swipe – will anyone top
his record?

Hours of amputations fragment thoughts
that reassemble body parts,
wool-warm and grazing
paddocks – rounding back through

the week, home to Vi's supple comfort, the kids
tugging his coat like lambs on the teat. Longing
returns, another slab
moves down the line. *Next* . . .

II.
Coming home from working the chain
with four pounds wage. His coat wrapped sound
against the soft applause of rain.

Through lamp-lit streets, runs for the train.
The memories in his head resound
coming home from working the chain.

The grind of blood-stained hours remain
tick restless through a windowed frown
against the soft applause of rain.

This double life, what loss? what gain?
can hold his own, will stand his ground
coming home from working the chain.

Fields flick past him, frame by frame.
Commuters hum through every town
against the soft applause of rain.

He reeks of sheep grease, scrubbed in vain,
her *Rocklea Road* sits, ribbon-bound
coming home from working the chain.

The track, a wooden leg refrain;
his carriage creaks and rocks and pounds
against the soft applause of rain.

Can't wait to feel her touch again,
to smell her soapy skin surround
against the soft applause of rain,
coming home from working the chain.

III.
Five boys lie still, fathom their father,
dreaming of his return this week,
then throw off bedclothes in a fervour –
Dad's coming home from legging sheep!

Dreaming of his return this week
has Mickey giggling acting the goat –
Dad's coming home from legging sheep!
Kev's got his hands 'round Gerry's throat,

has Mickey giggling acting the goat
Get the boxing gloves Ken yells
Kev's got his hands 'round Gerry's throat.
The baby's screaming hells bells.

Get the boxing gloves Ken yells,
before Mum gets the wooden spoon.
The baby's screaming hells bells.
Mum's muffled shout: *Don't speak too soon.*

Before Mum gets the wooden spoon
she's settling Gareth at the breast.
Mum's muffled shout: *Don't speak too soon,
Dad's train's at five, so be your best.*

She settles Gareth at the breast,
then throws up bedclothes neat before
Dad's train arrives. *Will be our best*,
five boys still lie, fathom their father.

– *Norwood Hill, 1943*

Offerings

I.
Ken's middle name
is his father's first – Francis. Frank
gardens on weekends, utters few words
spattered with curses. (He's no saint,
though the first to admit it.   Assisi's lore
draws him out.)

Sunday morning, Frank feels younger.
Hands in the dirt, he tucks flower seeds
and bare-rooted stock into beds out back
after a week on the chain. Rock crumbles
to clod, mineral iron in the loam.

Mick's pony bends the fence
to pinch apples from the orchard.
Timmy, the mad foxy,
yaps at Jacko escaped from his cage,
raiding the veggie patch again.

Frank ignores it all with quiet abandon.
Every creature needs a feed, he mumbles
to no-one, continues caressing the earth
to coax sprouts from the soil's marrow.

II.
Ken searches for birds' eggs,
walking to Mass
(on weekday services too). An altar boy
in dawn's half-light, he's robed in red
(black and white) like a prayer received.
Birdsong inspires unconscious notes;
he whistles response.

Each *Deo Gracias* day
he recites the *Confiteor,* charmed
by its yo-yo rhythm. He listens to Benediction
Wednesday and Sunday evenings.
Is mustard-keen to join the Children of Mary
and Holy Name Society choirs
(meeting every alternative month). Surely
he'll get his chance.

He craves
these rising antiphons
while his father is on his knees,
digging into the day-of-rest.
Only Frank's roses make their way
to church with the rest of the family
this brisk morning. The blooms
offer summer's faintest perfume,
the lightest withered leaves as sanctuary,
sanctification.

III.
Who went to church on Sunday?
Did I see you, Laurie Cartwright?
Sister Eymard snaps the class
to Tommy-gun attention
on inquisition Mondays!
Behind her, both hands grasp
a mist of feathers rising tail-like
from a cane handle. She waves
its metronomic wand
to conduct a tap tap rhythm –
each step each desk each
unanswered question
threatening discord, authority
endorsed by the black habit
tenting every inch of
her unimagined sex, bar
a face framed white.

She moves like a mountain
across the blackboard platform,
tassels abseiling from her middle
in swish swish sway, timing
instrumental to the natural order
of morning classes, after prayers –
Ken's own answered with
a bunched offering
from his father's garden

where snapdragons grow
yea high, all crimson,
sun-kissed pink and yellow,
prized as heaven-reaching gifts
fit for exchange – a fistful of blooms
for a cut-less day.
He stretches out an arm, raises eyes
like blue moons – *in sweet with her!*
long after their scent disperses.

IV.
Ken's elbow rests –
a wishbone across the desk,
careful not to knock
the ink-well's midnight depths. He dips
the nib, wrist poised above
lined page, forefinger and thumb divining
concentration. Joints clenched
to a blank point, he dives
into the first sentence.

He tries to synchronize the grace
of textbook copperplate,
smudges, slashes, starts again.
This time untangles letters, measuring
height and width by nature's breadth:
ticks *C*rescent moons, an *O*range loop,
slants gully *S*nakes, the *T*ree outside
his bedroom window.

Opening vowels, leaning on consonants,
his fountain pen strokes
a deft vocabulary.

V.
The only thing Ken loves more
than Handwriting and History
(and flying of course) is
singing. Next up
is Music. Sister Alphonsus
divides them.

Group one, start off
together now, one, two,
open your mouths wider
for a clearer sound.

She sits twisted, her wings
spread mid-flight; the left hand
tinkles sharps and flats while
the right hand
chops invisible necks
on divisible blocks,
pulsing out a beat beat beat beat.

Altos, your turn,
one, two, join in –
remember to yawn
to shape your vowels.

Her fingers pound chords,
black, white, then syncopate
a melody of sorts. Perched
on the rim of the stool,
she strains over quavers
and crotchets, sparrow eyes
gleaming at upright walnut,
tuned to task.

Sopranos go,
I want to hear
songbirds trilling
those honeyed tones.
Another bar, then . . . *three, four, tenors,*
your turn, I want your resonance . . .

Stop!
Too loud!
Who is drowning the natural harmony?
Kenneth McKinnon,
do you think you're Nelly Melba?
Mouth closed, Ken looks to his shoes
then side to side in the deafening moment.
The bell rings. *Dismissed*, Alphonsus shrills above
footsteps clattering floorboards. Laurie throws him
a dulled smile. Twittering children mill about,
usher him out.

– *Castlemaine, 2011*

Heroes at the Table *(Dialogue 2)*

My father jumps into song, (the pool
in my mind), brims with faces and places
he barely remembers,
rarely forgets

'"It's just a dream an illusion now"
*I was in the Norwood Hill Swimming Club,
we went all over the state, you know*'

'I didn't know'

'"It must come true, sometime soon, somehow"
*Johnny Mathis sings that song – do you
know it? He was a wonderful baritone tenor,
a well built chap, athletic, was nearly an Olympic
high-jumper you know – had a huge chest on him,*'

– I gasp for a word in his breath –

'*then there was Johnny Weissmuller, starred
in all the Tarzan movies, by geez he could
swim, had shoulders on him
like this –* '

Hands spread wide as a preacher's
or conductor's butterflying over
the table between us

'Oh we used to swim up at Bert Leister's dam
up in the bush, had racing blocks and everything,
the fathers dressed up to stir us up, you see,
you should've seen us . . . '

I'm struggling to stay in this line, caught in his stream . . .

'"All across the land dawns a brand new morn"
up in the mornings, we had a little dog we used to
take up into the hills around the old Ajax mines
near the dam there, where . . . '

I'm going under, swallowing his mouthfuls in great gulps

'we'd all try 'n dive like Johnny Weissmuller – a beautiful figure
of a man you should've seen him swan dive off
a cliff fifty foot or more in the jungle – pure magic, Tarzan
movies you know, we kids loved to go watch him
in a Saturday matinee
"It comes to pass, when a child is born"'

In this swim-song interval, I scribble
his script, drowning in the leviathan task.

– *Norwood Hill, 1943*

Laps

Dawn at the dam. Each stroke takes
Ken further away from roots
and clay. Muscles pull through
water velvet. Hips tilt left
right, arms brush sunlight, air
breathy with eucalypt.
In these practise laps is he drone
or dance?

He beelines deeper water; sun
flickers through ghost gums,
honey-thick upon the hull of
his vessel. This is the time and place
he can breach the calamities
of school and home. Find calm
in minutes paced in rhythm. His body
strength reaches, grows, as fluidity
draws him closer
to another dawn.

Carnival

I.
The Swimming Carnival's
well on the way when Norwood Hill
men go over the top. Frocked up
in sunspot polka dots, they bungle
the dam's shore-line raid – a whirlpool
of gaud and petticoat tails dripping
in mud.

Bosoms, stuffed to unreachable peaks,
sling pearls across chesty whites –
(cross your heart) in your face!
Ruby lippy bleeds into five-o'clock shadows.

Kids shriek above galahs,
brighter than flags. Wannabe-freak fathers
are all tweak and pull and twist –
ribs, lobes, hair, fingers,
in a head lock or Chinese burn.

It's all about scrabbling over
their younger selves (lined up at the blocks)
to clown about as high-board wobblers.
They slip, bombing the crowd
that rings the dam.

Men, grown
into noon-day lunacy,
make light of dangerously close edges.

II.
Ken's navy bathers hug his midriff,
underline pecs pale
but puffed on the way
to the makeshift blocks.
Each stride closes on stones
under tender arches.

He lines up with the lads. They lark about, wait
for their numbers to be called. The crowd's
stray caws and scarks start
to carry him away.　　He pauses,
stares at ropes lolling across the waterhole,
suddenly shivers
at the Olympian task. Cicadas tizz.
Bark and leaves drift like rafts.
Kevin's on the block next to him, hisses
you won't win, you're shit.
Ken blinks shadow sun, palms pray above, leans,
. . . waits for it . . . *Crack!* Pushes off,
sailing through glare; his own image
a ghostly double rising up
slaps him, dam-cold.

Decapitated limbs swirl
underworld, the throng's cheers
muffled above. He streams up, spurts
a mouthful through strobing strokes.
Left breath　　right breath
opponents straddle a shoulder,
an ear. He listens in seconds
for the end gun,
stringy-bark tangling
the maddening
splash whack effort of it – victory or defeat?

In the wake　　　a kookaburra's fading stutter.

Blue

I.
The kiosk sells tea to the mob.
Amongst magpie chatter,
a civility of teaspoons clink
in willow-patterned cups – a mosaic
of blue on lips and index fingers
    poised
with the promise of longer sips.

Afternoon sun freckles flesh.
Boys and girls flash mirror glances,
limb-to-limb, sidle up against
or into the queue for a second cup. Or
loiter behind dressing sheds
a spell, where apple-red shoulders
prickle heat and mirages ripple
gum leaves. Laura Brown's hair drips
rivers down the golden arc of her spine.

Sweating corrugations
in her tin-can hive, Mrs MacInerny's
pouring the tea. Sugar
ants swarm under thumb-crush, milk
warms to a yellow skin, and the scent of
spirit-laced fruit cake
ripens under marmalade glaze.

Ken can't take his eyes off Laura,
'til she looks up and he looks down,
spies a pair of wrens in the ti-tree bushes.

II.
Fleeting, the wrens strut
in a Spanish circlet. Tails twitch
full-fanned here here,
now flicked-closed there.   Again.

His royal head outdoes the sky,
extends to wings and rudder,
steers her attention.

Fleeting, she's gone
then reappears, swivelling
grain-flecked. Her neck
thickens, wings fold
in breeze. She eases closer,
withdraws, indifferent. Her fan flits
constant, the colour
of dust. She rims his distance
with a promise
of flight.   Again,

here and gone and here,
his Zorro mask bows, drops
wattle at her feet. Her eyes ring
orange before his golden altar.

Fleeting,
his violet attracts, deflects
her attention. His ardour dance
on her back, her outstretched wings
in exquisite breadth,
brown flap cloaked in blue.

Above, clouds nudge
the hillside. Florescence ribbons
horizon, glints
then is gone,
to nest or dance another sky.

III.
Later, the dam draws Ken back.
He lowers a shaky leg;
mud sucks him into the shallows.
His bulk ripples an aftershock.
A distant crow caws.

The water's cool in spots.
Wrigglers skim. Ken parts
their Lilliputian commotion,
glides to the centre. He's a cloud
watching clouds move, motes of light
just shy of breath. Head back, belly
up, he closes lids to the fading sun,
allows the dam to cradle him.

He opens an eye. A dragonfly's wings
filigree air.   He remembers
how Laura looked at him
today, Kevin's sly digs
about the swimming race he nearly lost,
and the one he did.

Smart aircraft, now the dragonfly
dips to the water's webbed light,
as if seeking stars of its own reflection
before it disappears.   Nothing else
writes the air but the purple
of dusk, and bird calls
he's yet to know.

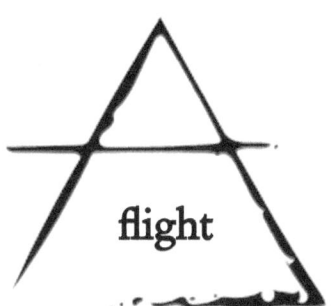

— *Castlemaine, 2011*

Musings from the Nest *(Monologues 1&2)*

1. His Bird Naming Speech

2. My Bird Forming Thoughts

'Birds, I know 'em all, their nests and eggs.

There's Great Bound Babblers; the Cat Birds'
are similar to a possum's nest made of twigs.
They have long eggs with a veined membrane,
both large and small kinds — bronzy grey eggs

>   *threads of bone-crusted carapace*
>   *hide breath fluttering inside;*

Native Goldfinches — like a Wild Canary,
Bronze Winged Pigeons
and the Wattle Bird, their eggs are pink covered
with dark red spots

>   *staring out of darkness, lukewarm spheres*
>   *are blood spattered,*

The Blue Crane, now he's pure blue
— you oughta see it

>   *shaded forget-me-not cobalt that deepens*
>   *like the dreamed sky's azure allure,*

(Hands splay, fingers front and centre over table.)

*He builds a nest over a dam, out on an
overhanging branch –
it's a stick nest. Tricky!*

*Blue Wrens, Tom Tits, Red Lories,
Ground Larks,
Plovers – now
they nest on stones in the creek beds and pretend
to have a crook wing
to lead you away from their young, like
the Ground Lark does, you see. Clever.*

> eyes pleading
> pearled moons in a come-hither dance;

*Kookaburras and Parakeets
build nests in banks.
The Laughing Jackass, now he's a 'rummen'
and you oughta see the colours on those parrots –
every colour you could imagine,
like the Rainbow Lorikeets;
Zebra Finches – White Nuns in the prickles.*

> jewelled inflections begin,
> a dawn song

*But the hardest of all to get to is the Crow, dark
as death,*

> erupts through cosmic effort, gasp-blue,
> alive

*in a nest ninety foot up. Kevin could get the eggs,
no one else could.'*

– *Norwood Hill, 1945*

Flight

I.
Dawn drifts in. Ken dreams
he's a cockie in a flock of kites
wheeling the horizon. Screeches
converse with tongues of sunrise.

He tries to decipher their speech,
listens for arguments in scarlet
flowers that burst with feast. Follows
the scent of their sounds, can just make out
feathered crests – like fingers waving
or curled to grasp a glass of air.
He salutes a brow, squints through light,
searches for his kind,
pillow and nest feather-lined.

Cockies keep calling. Alarm
his morning torpor
until he rolls over, nuzzles
another ten minutes under covers.

II.
Ken walks to school
ahead of his brothers, stops.

Hear that? And another?
He's heard this bird before,
glimpsed a leaf quiver
making presence
tacit.   The sound borrows breeze,
is nameless, formless
but for its ratchet script.

Perhaps it's a lonely myna
waiting for an answer.
He laments the untranslatable,
the shell of a wing departing –
from a nest or temporary perch?

Do its siblings listen
for the syncopated pulse
of flying creatures who beat
through the breathless body
of this world?   Is the song a sign
of avian hubris, immune
to risk? His own dumb hope
tunes frantic to catch
a glimpse
on currents, clouds.
Head up, he hears
another quaver *tick tick tick tick tick tick tick.*

III.
Now a warbler has hiccups, hiccups on speed,
another's hee-haw see-saws in out
loud with another's put-put mo-ped,
tripping a waltz beat to top hat intent.

The whole madrigal oils its machinery,
a warm-up crescendo with downpour applause.
Song lungs fill the sky's vast receptacle
fade in a minute to golden decay.

IV.
Ken can't help it.
He scrabbles bark for a foothold,
fledgling muscles limber as a possum's.
They've cut school
to snatch eggs, the possibilities
of prize, of schoolyard aerodynamics –

the swoop and pecking bravado.
Swings up in sunlight, grapples
shadowed maze,
white on bruise-blue on white eclipses
his skin, kaleidoscopic
as the sought cargo's speckled colours.

He's higher now.
Medicinal scent waters sight,
twigs make a nest of his crown,
scratch tiny forks across
cheeks arms legs bared
hairy with effort. He looks down
at the gang fisting his flight
like a chorus, *nearly there nearly there*,
hears the sea-leaves,
inches out, belly strapped to beanpole
the only division between
mortality and fall   nesting eggs, ellipses
each slow minute reaching.   Open

pouch mouth to house
the booty like stones, precious as
petals on his mother's cheeks earlier
this morning in frost,
waving them into the day's
learning.   He's swaying, now,

dizzy from height – floating on empty
there's only the weight of return.

V.
Eggs in a row wait for
laparoscopic surgery.
The jeweller's tool of choice,
their mother's darning needle

bursts the sac. Ken's
lips seal shell with a kiss,
blow slow, silent 'til
a gurgled whistle announces
aborted jelly. At its fontanel
and base, light fills the peephole.
Boys lean in, squint, in turn.

After, Kevin carefully places
the egg on the sill to dry. The sun
preserves the shelf-life
of its pristine womb; inside stripped,
bar a shade of yolk missed in the rinse,
haunting memories of flight
long after release.

VI.
Though uniform, each carapace
spatters a trace of species
beyond an eyeball's
sloughed stare.

These eggs are empty tombs
in glass coffins, or nesting
among socks and scarves
and cedar scents, drawer-warm
or cradled by hands, or
chaff-coddled in a Cohn's box,
draughts drifting through cracks.

Wherever these treasures rest,
they embody a mother's
paper-thin threnody. Her habit
regurgitating absence
– here and gone – even before
the feather-wisped act.

Shell

I.
Vi's sick of hearing it,
finds another lot, underfoot.

The boys' eggs infect every room
like giant insect larvae
or Christmas baubles, faded and forgotten
until their tug-of-war starts up again.

I'll not spare a penny farthing
to hear any more of your bickering,
boys – no more
do you hear?

The things just sit there, in the way.
I can't see the sense
in hanging on
to shells you've thieved then left.

Do you hear me? Do I have to
shout myself hoarse, till I've no voice
left?   Not a word.
Come and collect these eggs

now.   *I'm warning you.*
No stories or excuses –
I don't care if they're yours or your brother's,
Kenneth, Kevin, it's all the same to me.

I'll give you something
to fight about in a minute,
so they belong to no-one.
No-one, *do you hear?*

Broom handle smashes through
casing, shell, as if axing bones.
This purgatory act catches
like a swollen larynx. Their eyes stare,

helpless.

II.
Eggs (like open mouths)
in a swift few beats
are shards of bone and glass,
Ken's heart all over
the floor.

Cloud

I.
The Military March crackles through
HMV's golden gauze; PM Chifley, as if suffering
a cold, comes across . . .

Hiroshima bombed cshhh War cshhhhhh sh over cshhhhhhh

shhhhhhhhhhhhhh

as if

a dream,

as if

a cartoon bubble,

a cloud

of word rubble.

★

II.
That night in bed he sobs
pure blue, longs for the hue
of those beautiful eggs, like forget-me-nots
or violets in the woods (when Wordsworth
'wandered lonely as a cloud'
before he found those daffodils), or

a tint of sky or foreign things –
cobalt silk or tiles,
caught by afternoon wind or sun
before the Saracens came 'faster than fate'
blackening the horizon on Moorish soil,

or azure as . . .
Mount Gambier lakes
where volcanic vaults surely hold treasure
in grottos buried in blues unimaginable, or

a shade deeper than the Virgin's cloak
when crowned 'Queen of Heaven,' named 'ocean star,'
until the moon broke upon ink swells of midnight,

or . . . resting in gas-blue,
in an oven about to be lit . . .

surely not . . .   surely?

– Castlemaine, 1945

Flames

I.
Thirty convent girls, dressed up
as if meeting King George, in navy-banded
straw hats and matching gloves. Each tunic
starched as a nun's habit. They bandy around
the four new to Grade Nine at Saint Gabriel's.

It feels a bit weird to be the only boys, outnumbered
by so many skirts. Ken loosens, just slightly,
his tie and shirt, then remembers how much
he'll learn, his mother's voice reminding
how much it's costing. *But next year
I'll get my Leaving Certificate,
then the next, Matriculation,
then, perhaps, dare I believe, on to study
Aviation!*

Elbows nudge the four.
Voices hum about the room
like a hive, echo
off floorboards, tease with unpronounceable
enunciations. Flirtatious?
Or dressing them down, no doubt.

French first up! His tongue, trapped in primary
education, can't seem to conjugate
a single verb, or wrap
his mouth around the foreign vowels,
let alone utter a word
to those sniggering girls. No matter how
scrupulous his effort. But impetus begins
to grow from his red cheeks, and a secret

desire to kiss one. Laura Brown's
lips, like slivers of fig, part
as the class now begins
to practise Elocution.

A A A A   E E E E   I I I I   O O O (*Oh, I don't know
how I'll get through this*, he thinks. He can't
stop staring at Laura Brown's neck,
the wisps of her hair. His mouth is full of
cotton wool.) *U U U*
You, Ken, is it? Are you alright?
Er, yes Sister. **Fine!** To his surprise,
Ken almost shouts.
The nun glares. *Did you hear that?*
She asks the class. And then to Ken,
Your voice has a rich tonality!

Ladies, please! Sister Flavia snaps.
*Take up your books
for deportment. You boys may revise
your grooming rules, check shoes and cuffs
and collars and ties, until my final inspection.*

II.
Each morning, always the chores
before History, Language, Music classes,
never mind Algebra or Social Studies. Ken's keen
as rain to soak it all up. Flavia has appointed him
her apprentice fire-lighter. He hefts
and swings. Axe *cracks*,
dull on wood. Splinters dust the tepid sunshine.

The almond tree is losing its leaves, they fall
about him soft as silence. Damp lingers
on lips, on the wool of St Gabriel sleeves rolled.
Another split ought to do it, keep the blood pumping.

He brushes a tendril off his brow, checks
the damage. *Done!* Sister Flavia appears
to hustle him, miraculous! She glides over frost,
across the walled garden. Ken gathers an armful,
carts it in, dumps the load in the wood-box.

She crouches prayerful, stacks
a shrine in the hearth's black heart,
inviting his turn. Ken crumples
paper to fill its centre, strike-a-light
and *Behold – treasure brighter than Christmas tinsel –*
Veni Sancte Spiritus, she breathes.

As the morning wears down, flames
grow. Lesson bells clang.
Hands faces minds thaw,
washed in the glow of Flavia's instruction.

III.
Squatting staring at the fire one morning,
Ken prods a log and yelps in pain.
Sister turns to him, a wicked glint in her eye,
How would you like to burn in Hell, Ken?!

– *Norwood Hill, 1946*

Wick

I.
He waits across the hall, still as
a pew. A furtive fist nicks the corner
of his eye, another
as tears press and bloom
like leaves against stained glass.

A candle light stares out from the chapel
(where earlier Sister Flavia's face
flashed white). Flame's inkblot flares
in the darkness. He squints.
Drawn to the centre, haloed
in blue-white flicker, a moth.
Ken blinks – cannot look away,
is past understanding why he can't
stay and learn, why they can't
just let him be. His knees are numb
from offered petitions, a choir-full of
protests thinning upon Flavia's
words this morning,
*'You'll have to leave us, I'm afraid . . .
fathers need sons to work. We all have to
make sacrifices.'* Her alto tones reverb
across holy fixtures – virgin statue,
a heart-clutched saviour, crucifix –
as umbrage to his prayers.

He curls to the wall that night in bed,
his face caves in.   Branches tap dead
tunes at the window; he remembers the chapel,
the quiet of its wavering sanctuary.

II.
Where do these prayers go?
Wishing on this star
of light, he's cozened, cocooned
in dark.   *The candle is a symbol, it has to be*
– a sign of life

but gone to kingdom come. His father's
not-to-be words suffocate,
huff out education.

He's undone,
and confused. He's been a good son.
This riddle puzzles him. *Ironic*,
he thinks bitterly, *like the pun –*
*the longer **you** stand, the smaller I grow.*
As if the waxing flame
has become his father's tongue,
reducing him
to the wick.

– *Castlemaine, 2011*

Silence in the Kitchen *(Dialogue 3)*

*'My father burned my books, you know
- every last one of them'*

I wonder how
to conjure your absences,
fill your words . . .

I try to imagine being
there, being you
watching your father suddenly
jealous of your words-suddenly-wiser.
He, as if intoxicated
by the stove's little hellfire – shhhhhing
the stories, pushing their bulk into flames.
Blue tongues rise and rush
across the hob, script
withering inside.

I wonder how
that night, your mother's eyes
might have quietened your protests
like yesterday's news
folded on the kitchen chair:
Let   It   Alone
headlining every last one of them.

So many ways to silence . . .
So many ways to tell . . .

– *Norwood Hill, 1946*

Dante

Frank piles tome upon tome
in the orchard clearing.
Pages flap like doves
in shadows. His eyes flare.

Ken is a statue. He stares
into the Guy Fawkes pyramid.
It's as if his beloved books are revolting
from their shelves to play
stacks-on-the-mill in some strange night raid.

Novels, readers, poetry, history,
war strewn in an orgy
of leather bound and loosed.

One-by-one, torturous, they catch alight,
their guts spit, necks crack.
Ken watches ghosts rise, muted,
devoid of answers, of fight. He stands,
back straight, legs apart
as if taking root, surrounded by overripe fruit.

All that loosens curls, pregnant
with plume. All knowledge,
ideas, creations, disintegrate the same
in Dante's pyre, rise
and fall in fire.

His father's arm outflung in the act,
(across his face, the blank fact).

– Castlemaine, 2011

Resurrecting the Narrator *(Dialogue 4)*

'What was your favourite poem?'

*'The Ancient Mariner, oh
what a narrator! Now he
could tell a story.*

*He shot the albatross, you
know, and was punished by the dead
for going against nature,*

*and as his punishment and purpose thereafter,
it turned out he was doomed to tell
the story over and over
(to warn other travellers),*

*"With throats unslaked
and black lips baked"* –

*it's a sin to kill
an albatross at sea, you see,
because it's a sign of land.'*

'To lead you home?'

*'Yep, that's right, when you
lose your way at sea, "All at sea", you see?'*
You smile.

I smile back, *'I hear you!'*

*'That's what happens when you're
all at sea, you see – the bird
will lead you home.*

It's in that book I had at school: In Fealty to Apollo.
Not sure if I've still got it or not.
It had all the great poets – I could recite
'em all – but I loved the Ancient Mariner.'

'It's a favourite of mine too.'

– *Norwood Hill, 1947*

Delivery

I.
The idea of light taunts
darkness. Oak tree skeletons line
the track as if petrified. Step by step,
Ken's boots rustle through leaves
claret as old blood. Could be
off to church at this hour, but his father
lined this job up with Rasmussen.
Might as well have been Rasputin
with all the work he has to do. Will he
be pushing the broom about the bakehouse,
scraping benches or doing dishes, or
on the bread run today? Wonder if
he'll ever actually get to cook!

Nearer, the cart-harnessed horse
like a picture waits. *Hrumph
brrrr,* Ned's coat-close
nuzzle matts breath, warm
as rabbit skins on lino. Ken pets
his mange, shoves carrot ends into
his gob. Rassie's got
the bakehouse light wedged
in the doorway, whistles *Bread's
ready – c'mon boy, get to it.*
Chaff earth shit
stink as he walks towards the old man.

Furrowed loaves waft,
hatch honeycomb. He *tap taps*,
hears the hollow beneath crust,
tears off a scrap before shifting
the load from wrack to cart,
wrack to cart. Bread stacked,
dry and damp mingle
breath steam frost.
Hitch a leg up, reign *tit-twitch*
Ned into action, wheels creak
into turning
this daily bread
closer to delivery.

II.
Was this what they
meant when they said
'He was only a baker's apprentice
but oh how he kneaded the dough?!'

There's more homes than a baker's dozen
expecting to get fed,
delivering more than my work's-worth,
expecting to get ahead.

Half a crown to sweeten the deal,
lugging the weekly load,
daily bread by the wrack-full makes
a man rise along the road.

Cyclops

I.
Ken huffs, cheeks flushed,
spaghetti legs riding towards
an apple-full eve. Fields cross-stitch
the horizon; gold falls on green.

Orchard canopies
are closer now. Knees pump
past row upon row
of grass-flanked boles
leaning. Ten thousand crooked suns
orbited by a fragrant sea, and Ken.
The whorled fruit waits. He climbs,
reaches up, grasps
and twists; their necks
snap easily, a snack while he fills
the hessian sack
full as a wolf's belly.

In the tangle above, coloured scraps
flit, *screech scritch scritch*, a cacophony
calling through silence, the sloped
light. Here's a Cyclops eye,
another and another. Are they Rosellas,
Major Mitchells or Galahs?
Whatever they are,
one peck and apples
splat, ground ripe
with ruined fruit and bird shit.
Back aching, he stretches,
startles the flock. Wings *whop-whop*,
nearly knock him off, fly
to another harvesting day.

II.
Varied weather
at apple picking time.
Bike leans against
weatherboards out back,
frames his growing inertia,
triangular: from bakehouse
to Harcourt
to home.

Ken lingers,
stares down the ashen sky,
spittle pattering to shrapnel
on skillion tin. He sighs.
Might as well get on with it.

Three jobs, yes sir,
to stash the pennies, shillings
and pounds, to bake and cart and
pick and push the bike out and back
ten miles, storm clouds
smearing the brow
of Mount Alexander
in the distance. Hail numbs
his streaming face, the upward slant
of the ride. But still he pushes on
in boots that pinch
from too many winters,

while line by line, plot by plot
he learns the names –
Gala, Cripps Pink, Sundowner
and Granny Smith crisp
on his tongue. The tang
of reward more than
Mum's tart sauce or pies; a gift

tempering the tender bruises of his
sixteen seasons, once the leaves drop
like copper silver
green-gold promises.

– *Castlemaine, 1953*

Spacemaster

I.
Cost me six hundred pounds (after trade-in),
but aw gees she's worth it, Ken breathes.
A Vanguard Spacemaster, Phase 2!
He can hardly believe it's his
charging down the highway.

Bitumen steams after rain. The day gleans
a new brightness shouldering puddles
like a dislocated narrative.
Wireless croons Sinatra, The World on a String.
Snake-in-the-grass, this beetle has wings!
A wet-sleeved engine (it's a Ferguson tractor's)
and thin-wall bearings
with replaceable shells
give the solid chassis a spiffy new twist.
What a difference in performance –
a Spacemaster first!

A slick chrome strip joins his two-tone 'duck.'
Blue-grey duco flashes past paddocks,
the smell of tomorrow
hunkering into the trim: chestnut leather
seats and tortoiseshell dash.

Kangaroos graze wheat fields.
The sheen of husks, seeded in dreams
barely conscious,
manifest this any-new day. Lines overhead
electrify silent messages,
spread distance over time.

Through a half-wound window,
wind whips at Ken's cowlick,
cockies flap, just missing the windscreen.
Exhaust fumes haze in the rear view mirror,
Golden Fleece billboards
like a drive-in movie screen:
now starring *Phase 2*

purring into town, needle on half a tank, thirsty for more.

II.
Outside the Commonwealth
Savings Bank of Australia,
Castlemaine Branch, Mr Smith stands.

Smith swears by his credit authority,
this 'newly created institution
directing savings to the greatest
advantage of the people of Australia.'
The Commonwealth Act, his edict.

III.
Bank's bluestone
cornerstones Barker Street
and Hargreaves. Mr Smith manages
to confine his major function
to swishing back and forth
at the flies on his emblem of success.

He eyes off the crowd going about
their business, greeting them
coming in and out of
his establishment. Not bad
for a Friday, by his fly-by
bald-headed guess.

His waistcoat strains
at the button-holed fob. The street's full
of kids sockless in rags.
He wags a finger at their tease and snitch.
Watches folk walk or cycle, though
there are a few cars about, more or less.

Here comes a new-beaut Vanguard
purring to the curb.
Its duco reflects bluestone,
sheer as glass. Another customer? Can't
recall the driver's silhouette crossing
his parquetry lately, regardless.

IV.
Ken pulls up between
gutter and footpath,
engine hovers,
beleaguers Smith.
The window
slowly
peels
an Elvis Presley
cowlick
down
to baby-blue steel-grey
eyes staring at the manager,
and a slight turn of a mouth
monogramming
what might have been
a smile.

Smith's own grin,
monochromed
in shock
at the young driver
nestled, comfy-as-you-like,
in buckskin leather.

*Where did **you**
get the money to buy that?*

I saved and bought it myself.

— Norwood Hill, 1953

Incalculable

I.
Getting ready for the flicks, folks are
a picture of style. Mum's in her fur collar
and matching hat, Dad's wearing his
three piece suit 'n tie. Mum's worried
about leaving the house with Kevin
in there on the bed half passed out.

He's swigging liquor and cursing something chronic.
Mum wants him out in case he starts trouble.
*So you'd better get him moving, Ken. Get in there
and get him off the bed before he gets worse.
He's too heavy for your father to mess about with.
You're a good strong lad, so in you go and get him
moving; go on now, in you go so we can be off.*

Ken's feet are nailed to the floor with each step.
*C'mon Kevin, it's time to get up and get going,
Mum 'n Dad are going out so it's time to move.
Come on, so you don't cause any trouble.
Mum wants you to get going, out to the shed.
C'mon, get up will you? You're gonna get it if you don't,
and Mum 'n Dad'll be late for the pictures
and it'll be your fault, so c'mon.
Get up. You've got to move it.*

Next thing you know, Kevin swings around,
sudden like, and *ooofff*, rams his head right into Ken's guts.
You bastard, what're you doing? You fair winded me!
Kevin's up now and on Ken like a whippet.
*Stop grabbing me arms, you're pinchin' like a girl
you bloody drunk fool. Cut it out!* Ken gasps. *I'm just
trying to get you up so Mum 'n Dad can go out.*

Ken shoves all his weight into his brother's chest
to stop Kevin from knocking him over.
Ken's got a leg hooked under his, drops him,
thunk, on the lino. Now he's scrabblin' out the door.
*Thank God, Mum'll be glad as I am; but hang on,
what's that? Sounds like he's revvin' the ute. What the
friggin' hell's he doing? He can't drive like that!*
Then there's an almighty *CRASH*, and Ken's guts
are on the floor quick as he's out the door
looking outside himself
at his brand new Spacemaster Phase 2

rammed nearly in two.

II.
The cost is . . . palpable.
incomprehensible.

manpower x	7 years x	earning x
2 legs	64 hrs. pw	25 miles
+	+	+
2 wheels	15 hrs. pw (+ 4 hrs. pw/end)	53 miles
+	+	+
3 jobs	69 hrs. pw (+12 hrs. pw/end)	
√*domestic duties*	@	
+	bakehouse	@
	bread cart	£1,3s. pw
	apple picking	12s,6d. pw
	√*sleeplessness*	£6 pw/end
		=
		heart acher
		breath taker
		dream maker –
		for what?

4 wheels' worth,

a cinch if figured
incalculable.

A mudlark garbles
in black and white
brilliance. It stands
on one leg, the other is
missing.

- Castlemaine, 2011

A Pre-dawn Collision *(Monologue 3)*

*I cannot separate
your breath from this
nightmare, sweat and steam
and sob resonate
from that aching day.*

*I cannot separate
this hammock slung moon
in the darkness, soothing
broken sleep over your
daydreamt youth.*

*Nor can I separate
your grey wave on a sea
of discontent
made malleable by
your frenzied action,*

*I cannot separate
doing from being
in the shadow of your shine (shrine)
— up early, crashing about
the kitchen in pre-dawn collision.*

*I cannot separate
your be-bopa-luba radio
voice sung and swung
into the break-light
bake-house rhythm begun.*

Your engine growl and slide
over black ice bitumen
towards production and payment,
your under-breath muttering
summing it all up. I cannot

separate white from yolk,
edge from source,
wing from air, moon from dawn
to make this mean
something separate

you, my
father.

— *Castlemaine, 2014*

Stories from the Ashes *(Epilogue)*

I.
Side by side, the new and old sit:
the double-fronted buttery brick
and the miner's weatherboard
you were born in. Beside the house
that held your first scream,
first song, first meal, first tears, you built
your home, a verandah to shelter
a Christmas star,
grand stairs and a slate path
winding through standard roses. A juniper pine
at the centre of the three-tiered front lawn,
the monolith of Gainsborough Street.

Beauty and the worn remind the past
of its dreams. A rough-mown
nature strip, the green carpet
announcing your married life, the driveway
where your fifth car dripped oil stains
between the Canna lilies
before we six arrived.

In the cottage, Kevin
settled with your mother, never married,
continued to back the gee-gees at Sandown,
making his vigil to the Courthouse
Hotel a nightly drive, while Vi
prepared his evening meal.
Once Frank was in the ground for good, she left
the house to the one who stayed.
Because he has no-one else, she reasoned.
You couldn't understand the treason.

II.
You gave me your Webster
'double-brick' when you moved house,
I marvelled at the size of its sewn spine,
linen cover, frayed corners; its alphabet
thumb-nails curved into the pages
like gibbous moons guiding me to the words,
chameleon meanings.

Inside cover maps an 'Indo-European Family
of Languages', calligraphied on a tree. The first page
announces 'The New Twentieth Century Dictionary
of the English Language, Unabridged, Second Edition,
including etymologies, full pronunciations, synonyms,
and an encyclopaedic supplement of geographical
and biographical data, scripture, proper names, foreign
words and phrases, practical business mathematics,
abbreviations, tables of weights and measures,
signs and symbols, and forms of address. Illustrated
throughout'. Its details, laced with forbidden fruit,
mesmerized the hours, months, years of my youth.

Downsizing, you cleared out the books
that lined the lounge from one wall
to the other, from World War history tomes to
Readers' Digest, countless novels
and four sets of encyclopaedias:
Introduction to Science and the Universe
in a cool blue facade, a rocket ship pointing to the heavens;
the World Book volumes' gold-shouldered red
stood to attention like a troop of soldiers;
alongside, twelve apostles spouted politics,
and a compendium of faery tales,
nursery rhymes and ditties leaped
off their pages and into my bloodstream.

I greedily retrieved what I could carry
and store back at my place, on shelves
crouching in every room. *Take what you can
use* you said, passing on your beloved
books to me, your middle child, smallest girl.
I cannot separate the words
from yours, even now urging me to ask *Why?*

III.
I've got over 300 videos, you announce,
*All the good old films. I don't need the books
any more. You have 'em.* You hear about my poems
nearly every week. Start to retell me how
you couldn't stay at school like you wanted;
recite Elizabeth Goudge verse from a pocket
reader about monkeys and elephants acting the goat.

Their trickery tickles us both, their singing
and dancing about. *At least you've left your studies
'til after having your babies. There wasn't much point
any earlier*, you reason. *It's what makes the world
go 'round, and Love,* you grin with that twinkling
eye, testing my sex 'cos you know that I'll bite
and there's nothing you like better than
a matching wit. It's what makes you fly.

Mouth to Mouth

I.
The dewy seasons, spiced
and floured with fragrant mornings,
fill a   space   white
as a sheeted long table, a chair or two,
a roller and mixing machines –
stainless steel equipment
glints in tongues of sky
light falling
clean through
your Barker Street bakery,
chants a cha-cha
seductive as your two-step swivel
from bowl to bench

to flick a switch
to roll the dough,
and turn and shake
to roll again
expand and fold
and form a round,
again and again,
through dawn hours.

II.
Behind closet doors,
on proving shelves
mounds rise like mushrooms after rain,
yeast gestates
a cut-grass aroma,
waiting for your potter's hands

to sculpt or etch
cobs or scones or currant scrolls,
or Boston Buns,
sweeping the sweet patina back
and forth over ripe fontanels.

Tens of dozens of pastries and pies
are measured, made and dressed
for prosperity, each day leaving us
hungry for more.

III.
Just last week
you paced back and forth
pulling the goods from
electric ovens fired
with a twist of a dial.
You gripped the handle like a carnival ride,
hinged jaws
dropped with a knee-jerk. Trays slid out,
twenty-four pies with hissing hearts
laid on the bench to feed us
like blackbirds, mouth to mouth.

IV.
"Well bless my soul what's wrong with me"
Since you started this hip shaking, each morning
up with the birds, their chaotic choir, their whistles
sung as loosed moves – the stories keep on
through pipes a-calling.

"I'm itchin' like a man on a fuzzy tree"
You sing a bluesy tune, throttle rich as the tones
of a radio love song, scatting about the bakehouse
alone, cares scattered in a wrist flick, riffs
in a soft-shoe shuffle.

"My friends say I'm actin' wild as a bug"
In Hush Puppies, you howl
like a hound dog on heat, as the ovens
sweat it out steaming at the ears. You thrill
as the lift undulates, resonates

"oo oo oo, oo, I'm in love, uh, I'm all shook up"
Later in the evening (all the music seeping through),
between the meal and a movie, you
leaf through the pages of a history book
you've kept, wondering – what's next?

Notes

Songs from the Kitchen *(Prologue)*

p. 15: *Twas Mulga Bill from Eaglehawk that caught the cycling craze* is a line from the ballad 'Mulga Bill's Bicycle', by A. B. 'Banjo' Paterson, 1846.

p. 16: Hobyars are fictional creatures from an old Scotch nursery tale.
The Razor's Edge, Edward Goulding (dir), 20th Century Fox, 1944; *Random Harvest*, Meryn Leroy (dir), MGM, 1942; *Born Yesterday*, George Cukor (dir), Columbia Pictures, 1950; *Hobson's Choice*, David Lean (dir), United Artists, 1954; *Tarzan the Apeman*, W. S. Van Dyke(dir), MGM, 1932; *Shane*, George Stevens (dir), Paramount, 1953. *Boys' Own* refers to various magazine series published for pre-teen and teenage boys in the UK and US between the mid-19th and mid-20th centuries.

p. 17: *Oh Danny Boy* and 'pipes [attuned to re]calling' are lines rearranged from the traditional Irish song, 'Danny Boy', lyric by Frederic Weatherly, 1910.

Icarus

p. 18: Manpower was the work brigade commissioned in 1942 by the Australian government to help pool and support Australia's war effort.

Blood

p. 21: Two-tooth is a cut of meat from a two year old sheep.

Labour

p. 31: 'bubble trouble bubble' alludes to Shakespeare's line from the three witches brewing a spell in *Macbeth,* 1606.

p. 32: 'Tim's a king' is an intertextual reference to Jacko the ferret, described as 'a king' in Rabbits, p. 22.

Chain

p. 35: Frank Mc was a first legger: one who cut the first leg from the sheep carcass. Frank held the Australian record for legging a sheep (nine seconds) in the 1930s at Angliss' Meatworks, Footscray, (sold in 1934 to Vesteys, a British firm who introduced the chain slaughtering system).
Healy, Chris (ed.), *The Lifeblood of Footscray: Working lives at the Angliss Meatworks,* Melbourne's Living Museum of the West, Melbourne, 1986.
p. 36: Four pounds was the average wage of a 1930s abattoir butcher in Victoria.
Rocklea Road is a brand of confectionary from Darryll Lea's chocolate factory, Melbourne, 1940.
p. 37: 'Five boys lie still, fathom their father' inverts *Full fathom five thy father lies*, Ariel's song of transformation through death in *The Tempest* by Shakespeare, 1610. Cross-references Sylvia Plath's poem, 'Full Fathom Five', inspired by Shakespeare's characters and her own tortured relationship with her father. Cf: Plath's poem 'Daddy'. Highlights and twists K. Mc's family tumult.

Offerings

p. 38: Saint Francis of Assisi founded the Franciscan order of the Catholic Church in 1210, dedicated to poverty, charity and respecting nature, qualities avid in Frank.
p. 39: 'Confetior' is the Prayer of Contrition in the Catholic Order of Mass.

Heroes at the Table *(Dialogue 2)*

pp. 47 & 48: Song lyrics quoted from 'When a Child Is Born', by Johnny Mathis, 1976.

Blue

p. 52: Laura Brown is modelled on K. Mc's fascination with *Lorna Doone*, heroine and title of the novel by Richard Doddridge Blackmore, 1876; a tale of love, revenge and rivalry based on historical characters.

Flight

p. 64: Cohn's box refers to Cohn's Brothers cordial, fruit preserves and beer, established during the Gold Rush in Sandhurst. Cohn's products were packed in a wooden box stamped with the company logo.
'here and gone' is an intertextual reference to the Jenny wren's dance in Blue, p. 53.

Cloud

p. 67: *I wandered lonely as a cloud* is the first line and title of the poem by William Wordsworth, 1807.
Faster than Fate is a line from the poem, 'War Songs of the Saracens', by James Elroy Flecker, 1915. K. Mc would often recite this poem.
p. 68: Mt Gambia, South Australia, is home to the volcanic Crater Lakes, including the Blue Lake which is known for its mysterious turquoise depths changing hue with the seasons. K. Mc spoke of his visits to these lakes.
Queen of Heaven ... ocean star lyric is from the Catholic prayer and hymn, 'Hail Holy Queen', composed in the Middle Ages by an unknown source.
'gas-blue' alludes to the Holocaust genocide at Auschwitz (1941-1945), the devastating vastness of past, public horror alongside personal grief.
Many of the blue images in Cloud are intertextual, referring back to 'Musings from the Nest *(Monologues 1 & 2)*', pp: 59 & 60, depicting how quickly life (and hope) can change.

Flames

p. 73: *veni sancte spiritus*, 'Come, Holy Spirit', is a Roman Catholic Pentecostal invocation from the Acts of the Apostles, NT, *Jerusalem Bible*. It is also a hauntingly beautiful Gregorian Taize chant, published as one of four medieval sequences in *Missale Romanum*, 1570.

Wick

p. 77: 'not-to-be' mimics Hamlet's famous soliloquy, by William Shakespeare, 1599.
'The longer you stand the shorter I grow' are lines rephrased from 'Little Nancy Etticoat', a traditional English nursery rhyme, (from 'a compendium of faery tales', *Stories from the Ashes*, p. 100). In full: *Little Nancy Etticoat/ wears a white petticoat/ and a red nose/ the longer she stands/ the smaller she grows.*

Silence in the Kitchen *(Dialogue 3)* & Dante

pp. 78 & 79: Both poems allude to Nazi book burnings and allied censorship from 1933-1946, particularly Kristallnacht, 1938, linking the personal to international horror and disbelief.

Resurrecting the Narrator *(Dialogue 4)*

p. 80: *With throats unslaked/ and black lips baked* is from 'The Rime of the Ancient Mariner', by Samuel Taylor Coleridge, 1834.

Delivery

p. 82: *The idea of light* is a line from 'Echo Poems/ Mrs–: 1 Scald', from *Press Release*, a collection by Lisa Gorton, Giramondo, Artarmon, 2007.

Spacemaster

p. 87: Harold Arlen and Ted Koehler composed 'The World on a String', 1932, repopularised by Frank Sinatra in 1953.
The lines 'a wet sleeved engine (a Ferguson tractor's)/ and thinwall bearings with replaceable shells' are paraphrased from the Standard Classic Cars website, and K. Mc's knowledge of Vanguard

engines, 2012.

'Two-toned duck' was the colloquial expression used to describe two-toned paintwork on a car.

p. 88: Golden Fleece refers to a mid-twentieth century Australian petroleum company, and the Greek myth of Jason and the Argonauts.

Quote is from the *Commonwealth Bank (Interpretation) Act*, National Archives of Australia, 1953.

Stories from the Ashes *(Epilogue)*

p. 100: Quote from McKechnie, Jean L. (gen. supervising ed), *Webster's New Twentieth Century Dictionary*, The World Publishing Company, Cleveland and New York, 1960.

Mouth to Mouth

pp. 103 & 104: The lines 'twenty-four pies with hissing hearts ... like blackbirds' plays with the old English nursery rhyme, 'Sing a Song of Sixpence', origin unknown.

Lyrics quoted are from the first verse of 'All Shook Up', by Otis Blackwell and Elvis Presley, 1957.

Hush Puppies are a shoe brand made by Australian company Grosby.

Late in the evening (all the music seeping through) lyric is from the song, 'Late in the Evening', by Paul Simon, 1979.

Prologue, Dialogues, Monologues and Epilogue sections include verbatim and slightly paraphrased informal interviews between the narrator (author) and her subject (K. Mc), conducted in Castlemaine, Victoria, during 2011 and 2014 respectively.

Some of the dialogue in the body of the narrative is also verbatim from these interviews and previous stories as told by K. Mc.

Appendix

Violet McShanag
(nee Ablett)
1920s

Frank & Vi McShanag,
at K Mc's wedding,
Castlemaine Botanical
Gardens, 1959

Daniel jnr, Daniel snr & worker,
McShanag's Family Butchers, Graham St, Winter's Flat, 1914.
(Castlemaine Historical Society Inc, VCMHS, 1999, 241K)

Frank & his brother, Imperial Hotel balcony, Castlemaine, 1920s
(Castlemaine Historical Society Inc, VCMHS, 1999, 241K)

K. Mc, St Mary's Primary School,
Castlemaine, 1940

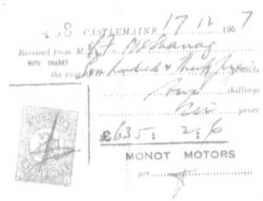

Spacemaster Phase 2 receipt,
Castlemaine, 1957

K. Mc, Castlemaine,
early 1950s

K. Mc & his Spacemaster, Guildford, 1958

Rasmussen's Bakery boys, inc K. Mc (top right),
Graham St, Castlemaine, late 1940s/ early 1950s

Ovens and rolling machine,
Barker St bakehouse, 2011

Keith preparing his window
at McShanag's Pie Shop, Barker St, Castlemaine, 2001
(Clare McShanag - clarefotografie 2001)

K. Mc & author's family home,
Gainsborough St, Norwood Hill, built early 1960s,
alongside his childhood home (1920s)

Tru S. Dowling is a Bendigo mother, poet, performer, freelance writer and editor. She has taught Professional Writing & Editing at Victoria University, Bendigo Kangan Institute and privately for over 16 years. Pre-occupations include hospitality, volunteer counselor, and singer-songwriter for folk band *The Wagtales*. Her poems have been awarded, read or published in Australia, Ireland, the UK and USA, credited to *Eureka Street*, *Famous Reporter*, *Poetry Monash*, *Blue Giraffe*, *Scintillae*, *Tamba*, *Offset*, *Skylight 47*, *Antipodes*, *Poetica Christi Press*, *Melbourne Poets' Union*, *FAW* and *Torriano's*. Tru has appeared at various writers' festivals and exhibited her work alongside artists and musicians. Community projects, social justice, nature, the dialogical and relational inspire her writing. *Memoirs of a Consenting Victim* (Mark Time Books, 2011) is Tru's first poetry collection; her latest manuscript is *Canopy*.

www.ingramcontent.com/pod-product-compliance
Lightning Source LLC
Chambersburg PA
CBHW020427010526
44118CB00010B/461